W9-AZS-134

SAMURAI

Written By Don McLeese

Illustrated By Chris Marrinan

ROURKE PUBLISHING

Vero Beach, Florida 32964

www.rourkepublishing.com

Edited by Katherine M. Thal
Illustrated by Chris Marrinan
Art Direction and Page Layout by Renee Brady

Photo Credits: © julioechandia & 45RPM: Title Page, 4, 5, 26, 27, 28, 29, 30, 31, 32; © Library of Congress: 26, 28; © Radu Razvan: 27

Library of Congress Cataloging-in-Publication Data

McLeese, Don.
 Samurai / Don McLeese.
   p. cm. -- (Warriors graphic illustrated)
 Includes bibliographical references and index.
 ISBN 978-1-60694-435-6 (alk. paper)
 ISBN 978-1-60694-544-5 (soft cover)
1. Samurai--Juvenile literature. 2. Japan--History--Juvenile literature. 3. Graphic novels. I. Title.
 DS827.S3M38 2010
 952'.02--dc22
                        2009020497

Printed in the USA

CG/CG

ROURKE PUBLISHING

www.rourkepublishing.com - rourke@rourkepublishing.com
Post Office Box 643328 Vero Beach, Florida 32964

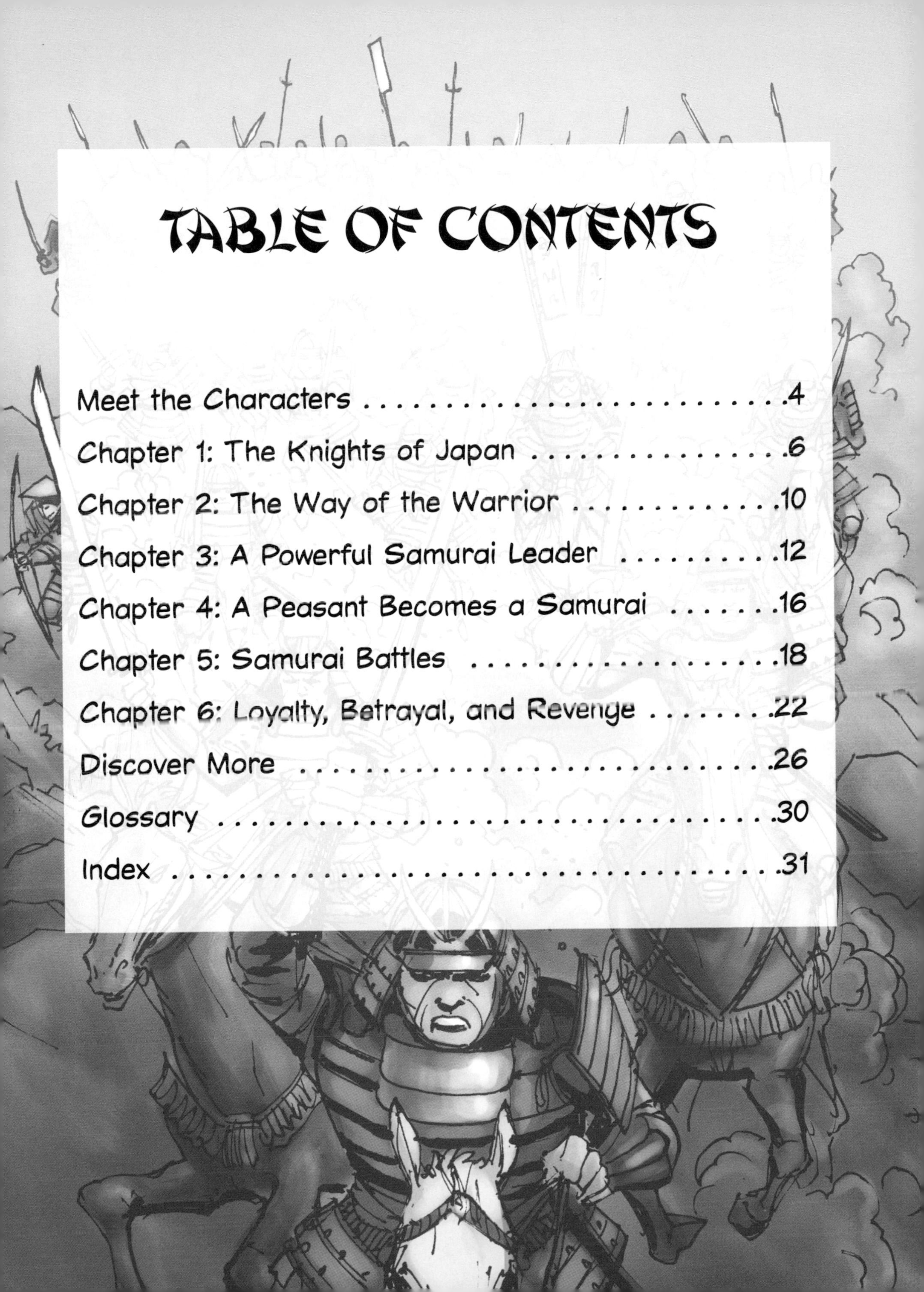

TABLE OF CONTENTS

Oda Nobunaga

The most powerful samurai leader from the famous Oda clan. In the 1500s, the Oda clan split into sides, which became enemies. Two of Oda Nobunaga's brothers led rebellions against him, and his victory over them made him even more powerful.

Toyotomi Hideyoshi

The son of a poor woodcutter, he became a great samurai leader, even though most samurai were born into noble samurai families. He was one of the most faithful followers of Oda Nobunaga.

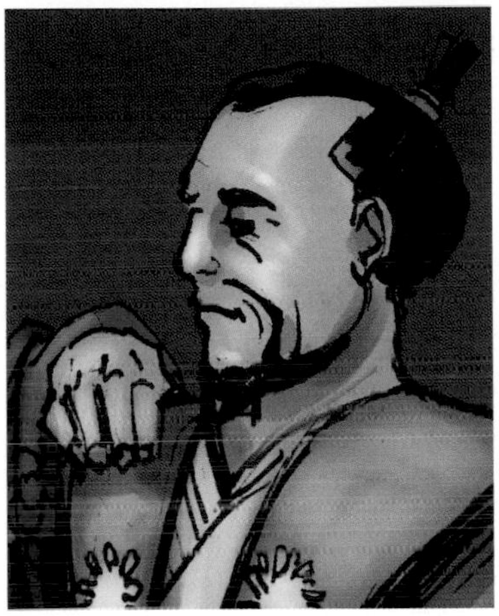

Akechi Mitsuhide

He was another follower of Oda Nobunaga, but he was jealous of his leader's power. He led a rebellion against Nobunaga, which led to a showdown with Toyotomi Hideyoshi. Previously on the same side, they became rivals.

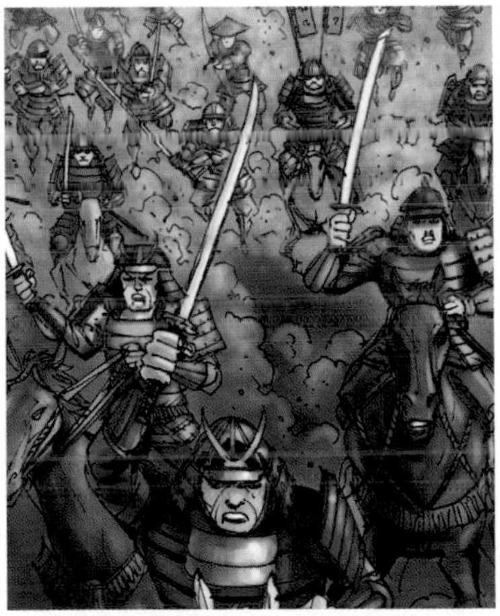

Samurai Army

The samurai army consisted of warriors who pledged total allegiance to protecting their master and his lands. Most of the warriors were born into samurai families, but a few were recruited based on bravery or skills. During different periods of time, a leader was called a shogun or daimyo.

Note: Although this story is fiction, the characters are based on real people and true events that they experienced in their lives.

THE KNIGHTS OF JAPAN

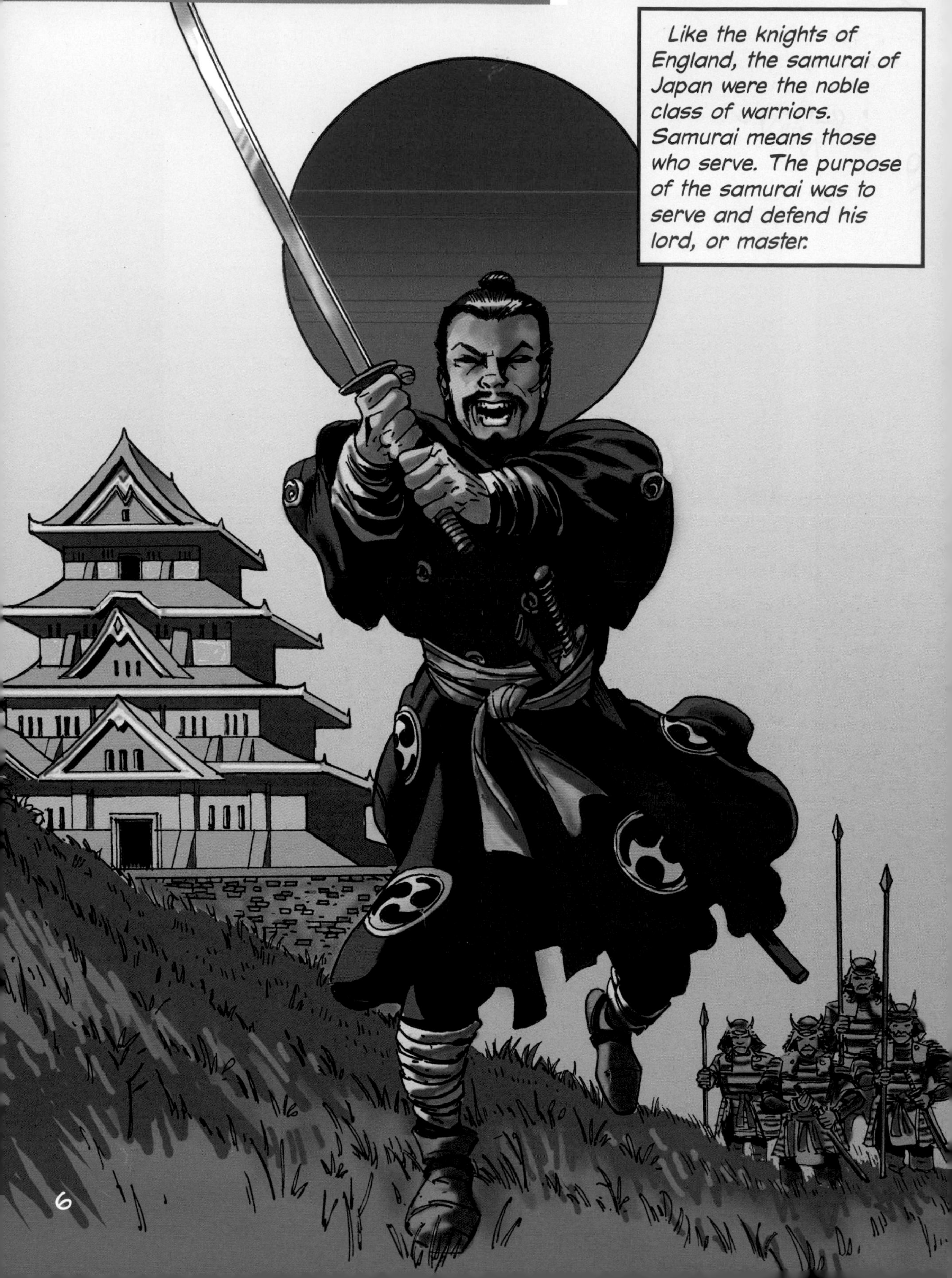
Like the knights of England, the samurai of Japan were the noble class of warriors. Samurai means those who serve. The purpose of the samurai was to serve and defend his lord, or master.

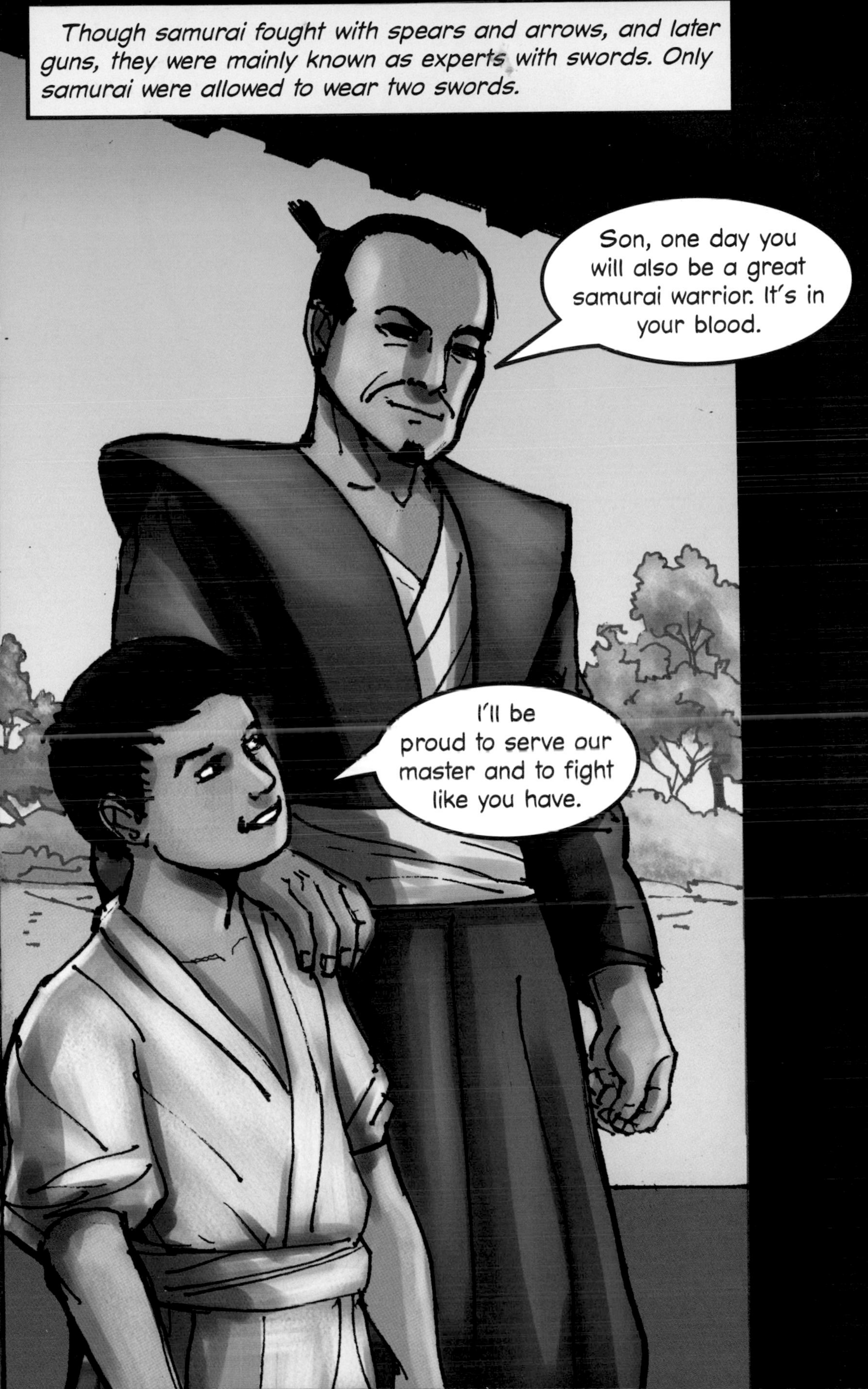
Though samurai fought with spears and arrows, and later guns, they were mainly known as experts with swords. Only samurai were allowed to wear two swords.
Son, one day you will also be a great samurai warrior. It's in your blood.
I'll be proud to serve our master and to fight like you have.

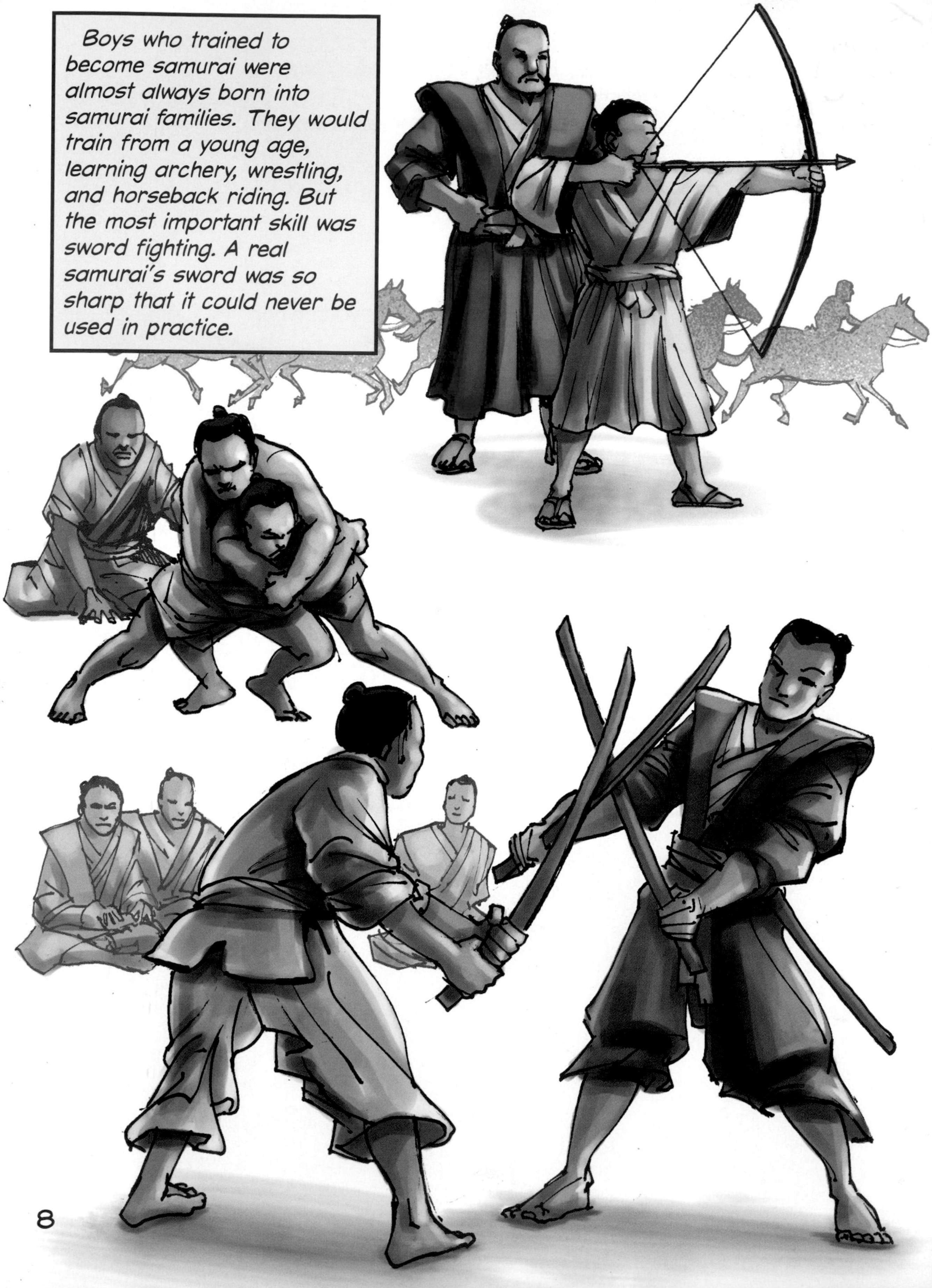
Boys who trained to become samurai were almost always born into samurai families. They would train from a young age, learning archery, wrestling, and horseback riding. But the most important skill was sword fighting. A real samurai's sword was so sharp that it could never be used in practice.

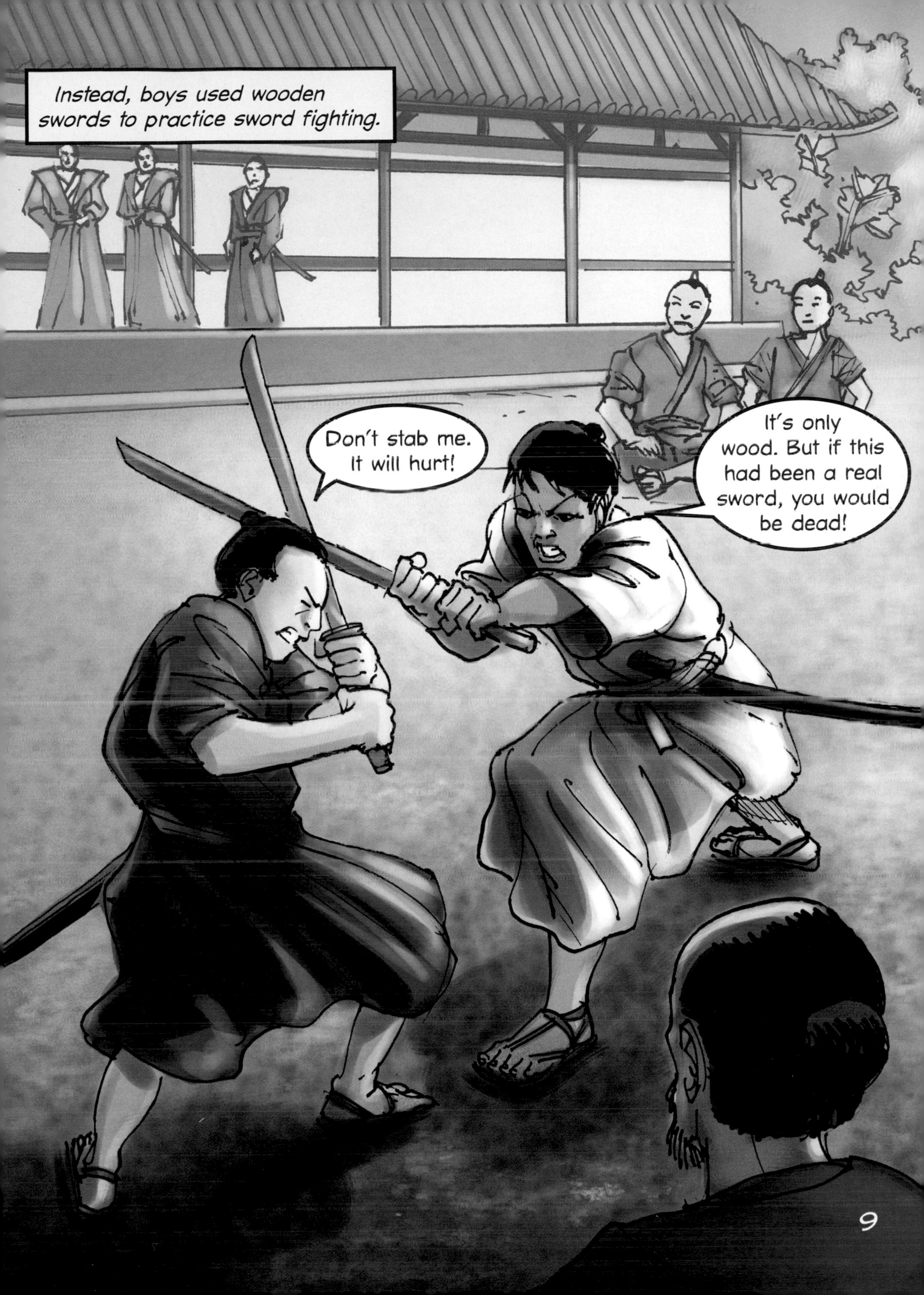

Instead, boys used wooden swords to practice sword fighting.
Don't stab me. It will hurt!
It's only wood. But if this had been a real sword, you would be dead!

THE WAY OF THE WARRIOR

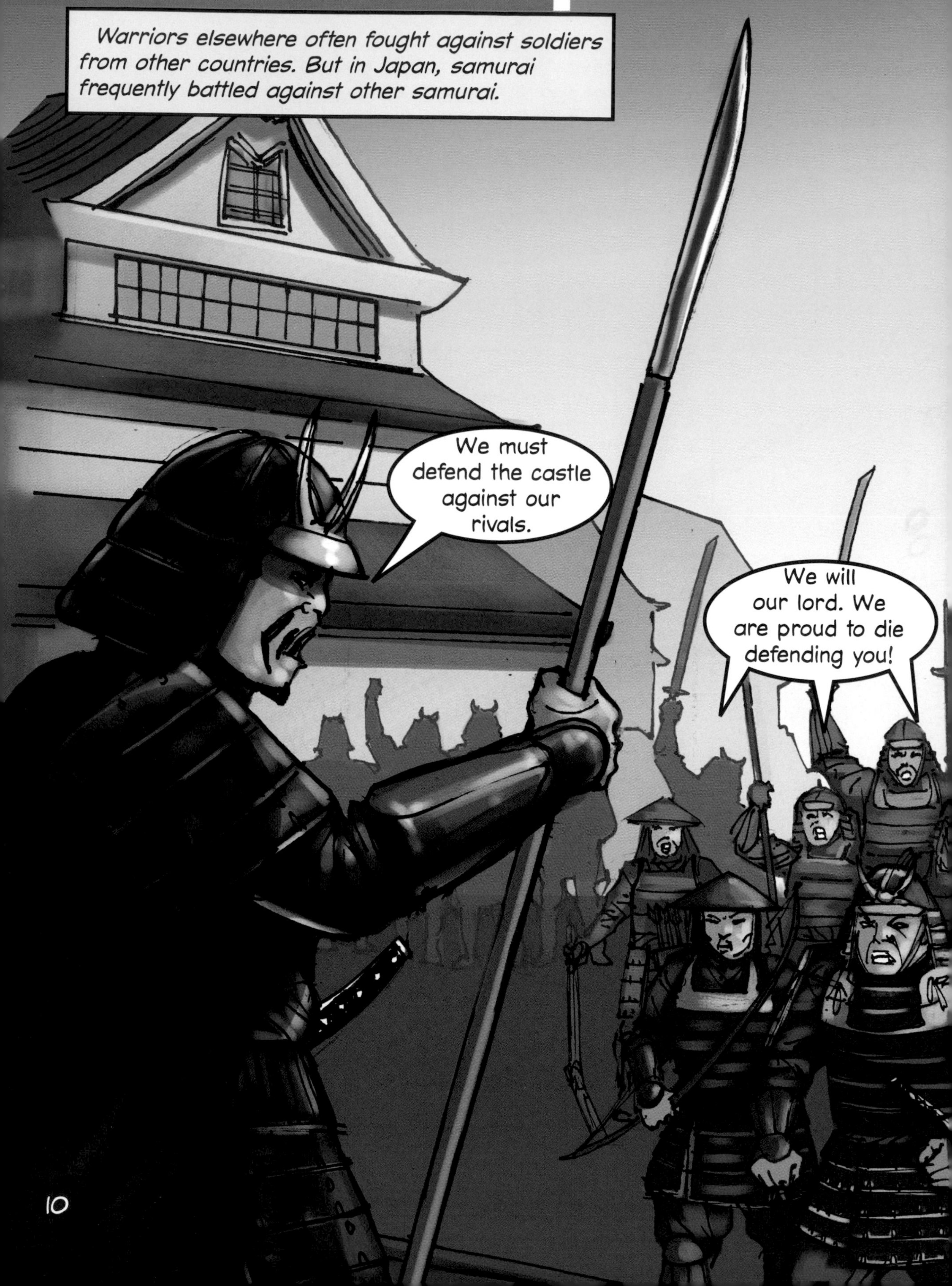
Warriors elsewhere often fought against soldiers from other countries. But in Japan, samurai frequently battled against other samurai.
We must defend the castle against our rivals.
We will our lord. We are proud to die defending you!

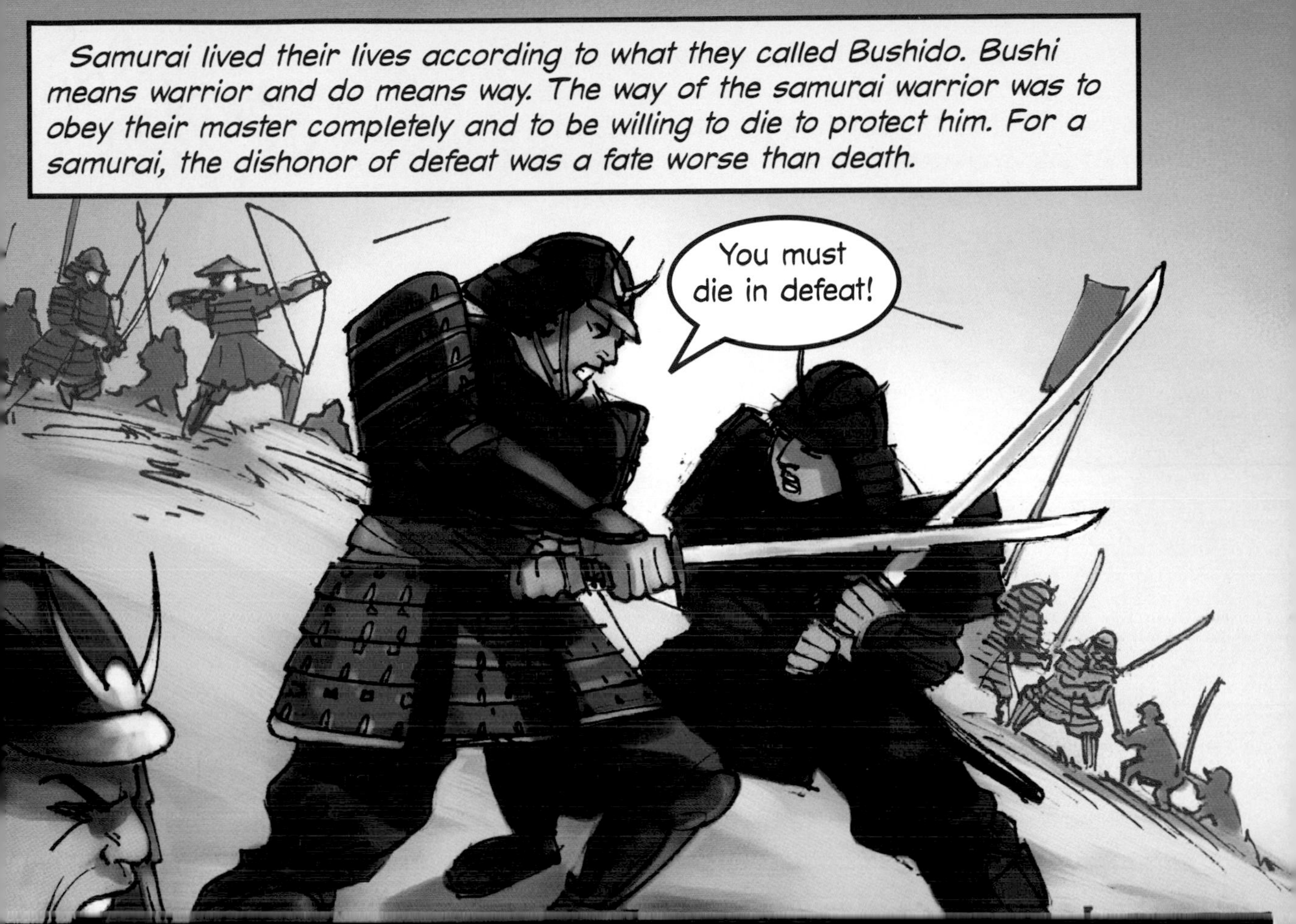
Samurai lived their lives according to what they called Bushido. Bushi means warrior and do means way. The way of the samurai warrior was to obey their master completely and to be willing to die to protect him. For a samurai, the dishonor of defeat was a fate worse than death.
You must die in defeat!

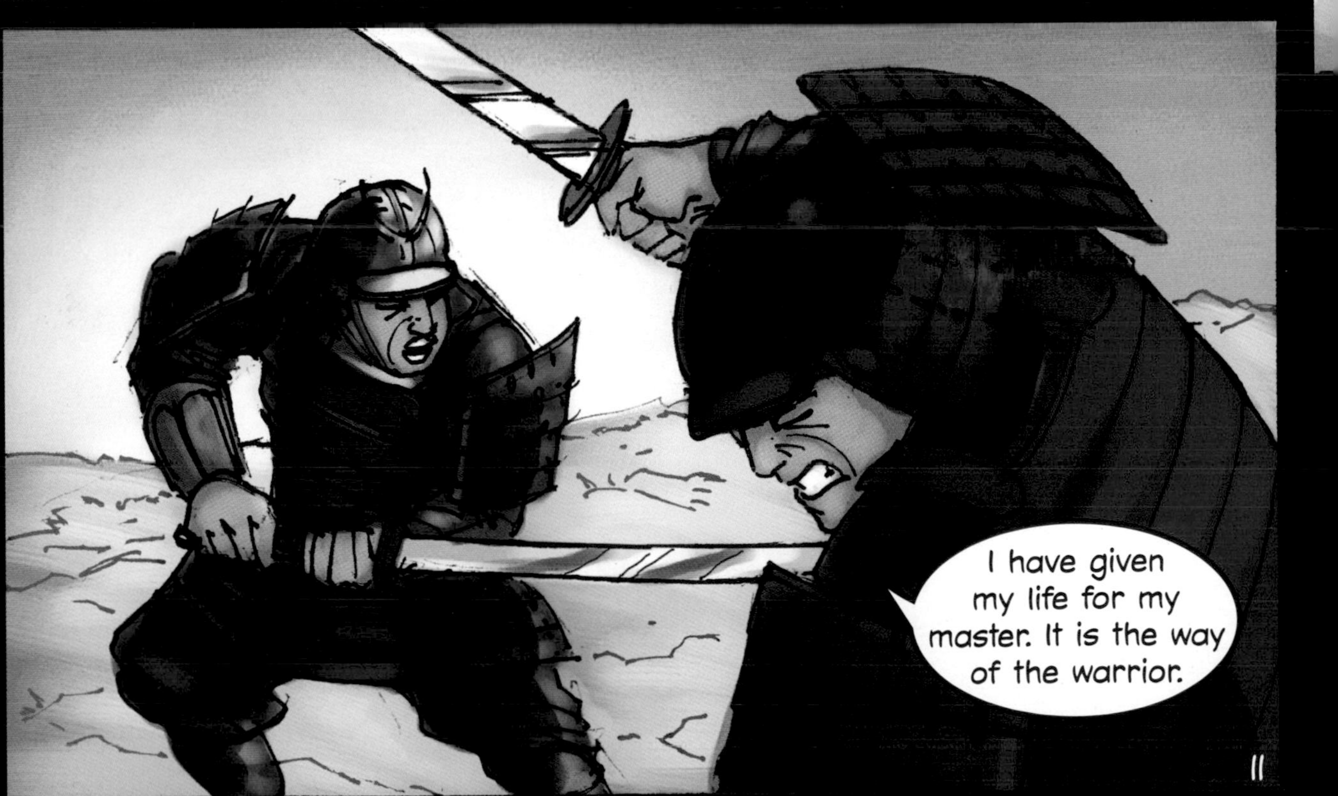
I have given my life for my master. It is the way of the warrior.

A POWERFUL SAMURAI LEADER

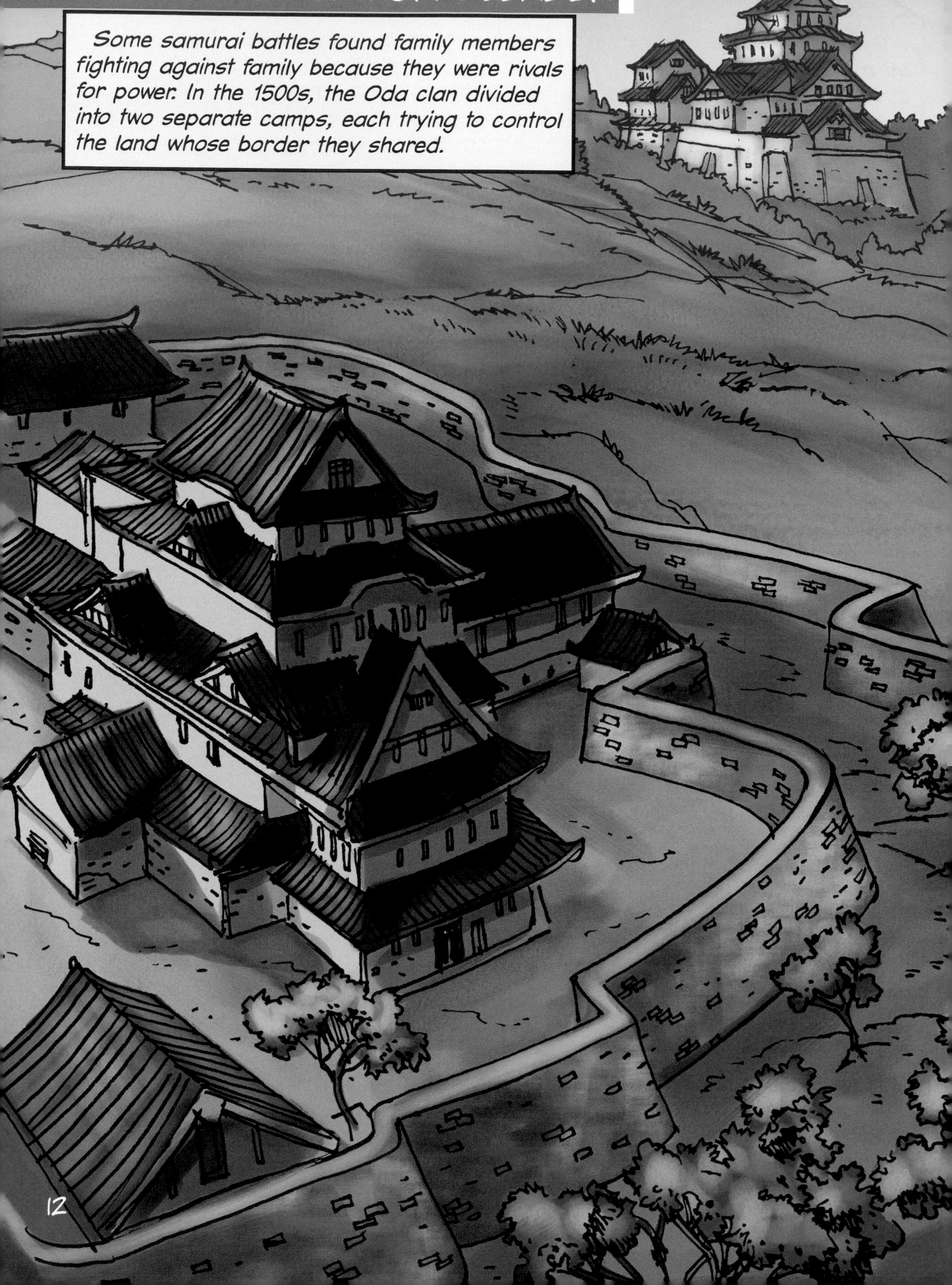
Some samurai battles found family members fighting against family because they were rivals for power. In the 1500s, the Oda clan divided into two separate camps, each trying to control the land whose border they shared.

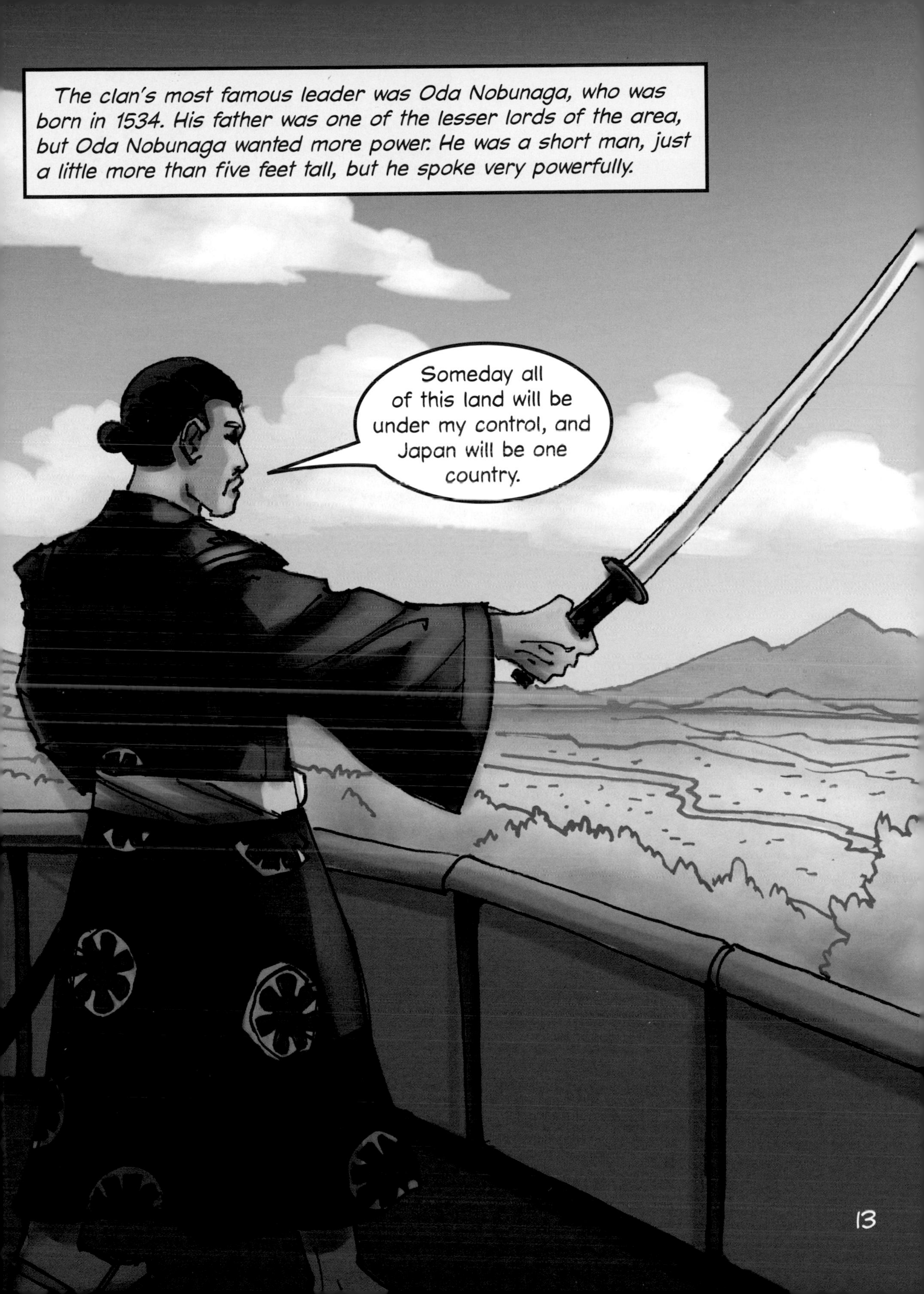
The clan's most famous leader was Oda Nobunaga, who was born in 1534. His father was one of the lesser lords of the area, but Oda Nobunaga wanted more power. He was a short man, just a little more than five feet tall, but he spoke very powerfully.
Someday all of this land will be under my control, and Japan will be one country.

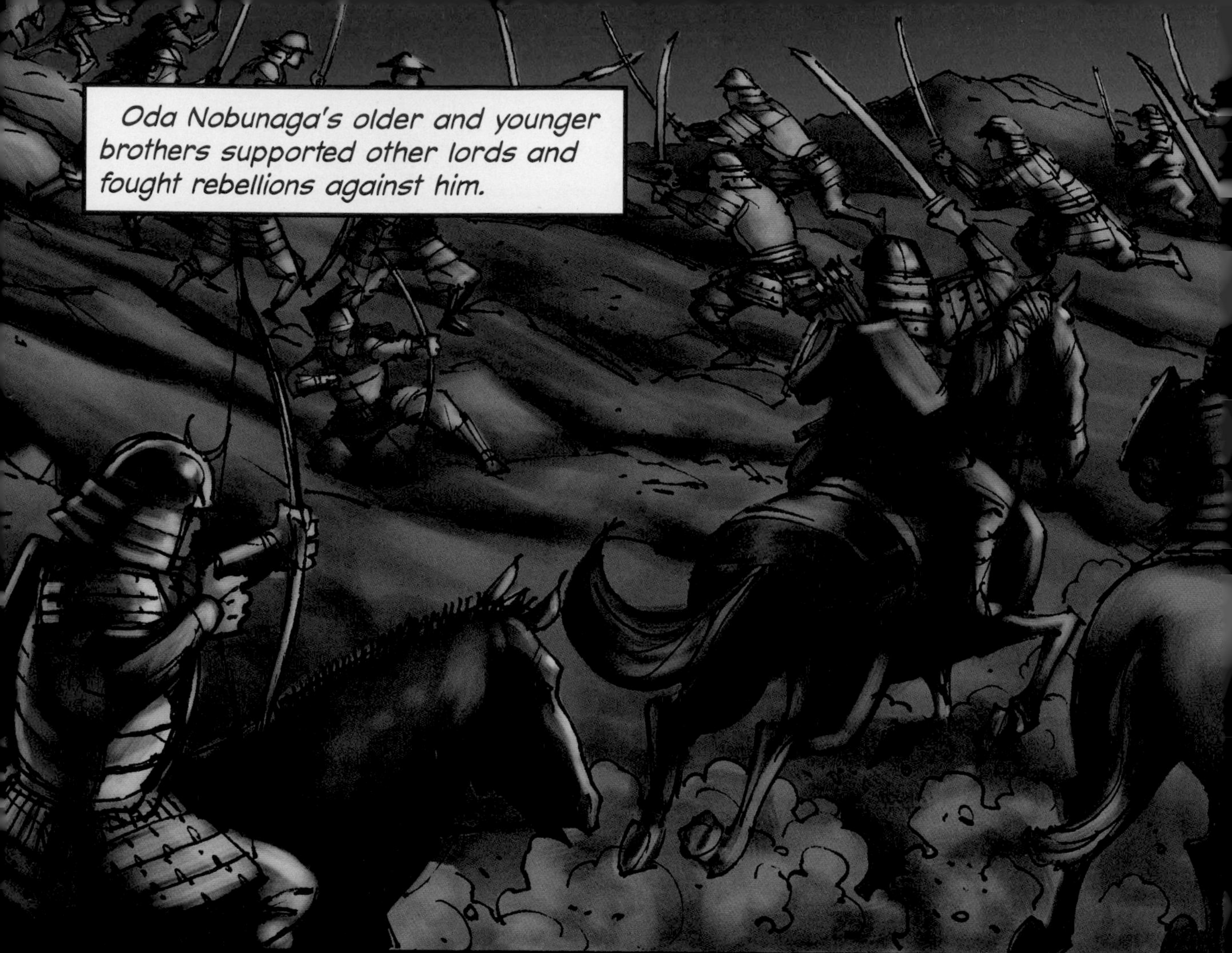
Oda Nobunaga's older and younger brothers supported other lords and fought rebellions against him.

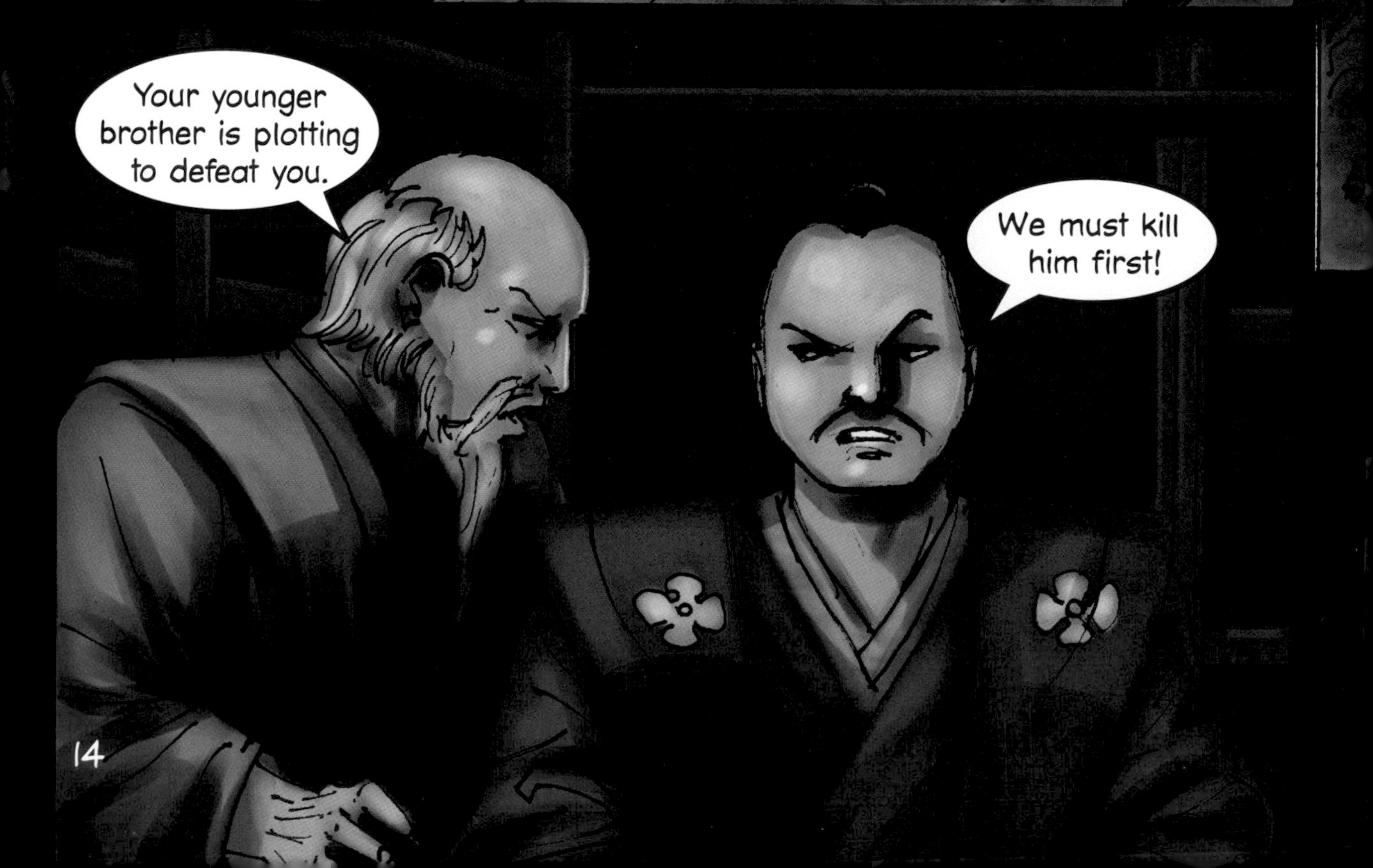
Your younger brother is plotting to defeat you.
We must kill him first!

Everyone became more fearful of Oda Nobunaga upon witnessing his brother's execution.
We must obey our great samurai leader!
If he is able to kill his own brother, he is very capable of killing us too.

A PEASANT BECOMES A SAMURAI

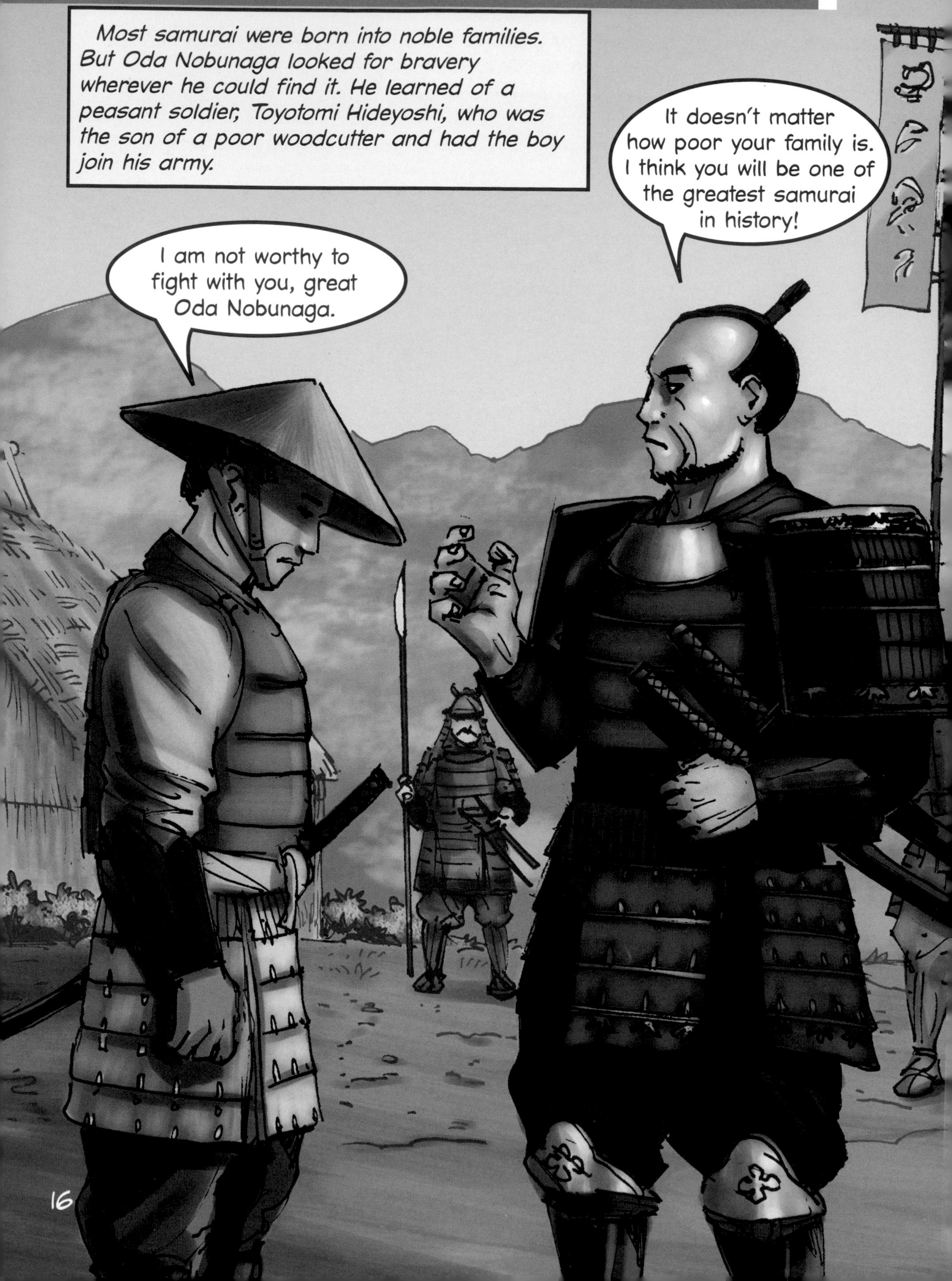
Most samurai were born into noble families. But Oda Nobunaga looked for bravery wherever he could find it. He learned of a peasant soldier, Toyotomi Hideyoshi, who was the son of a poor woodcutter and had the boy join his army.
I am not worthy to fight with you, great Oda Nobunaga.
It doesn't matter how poor your family is. I think you will be one of the greatest samurai in history!

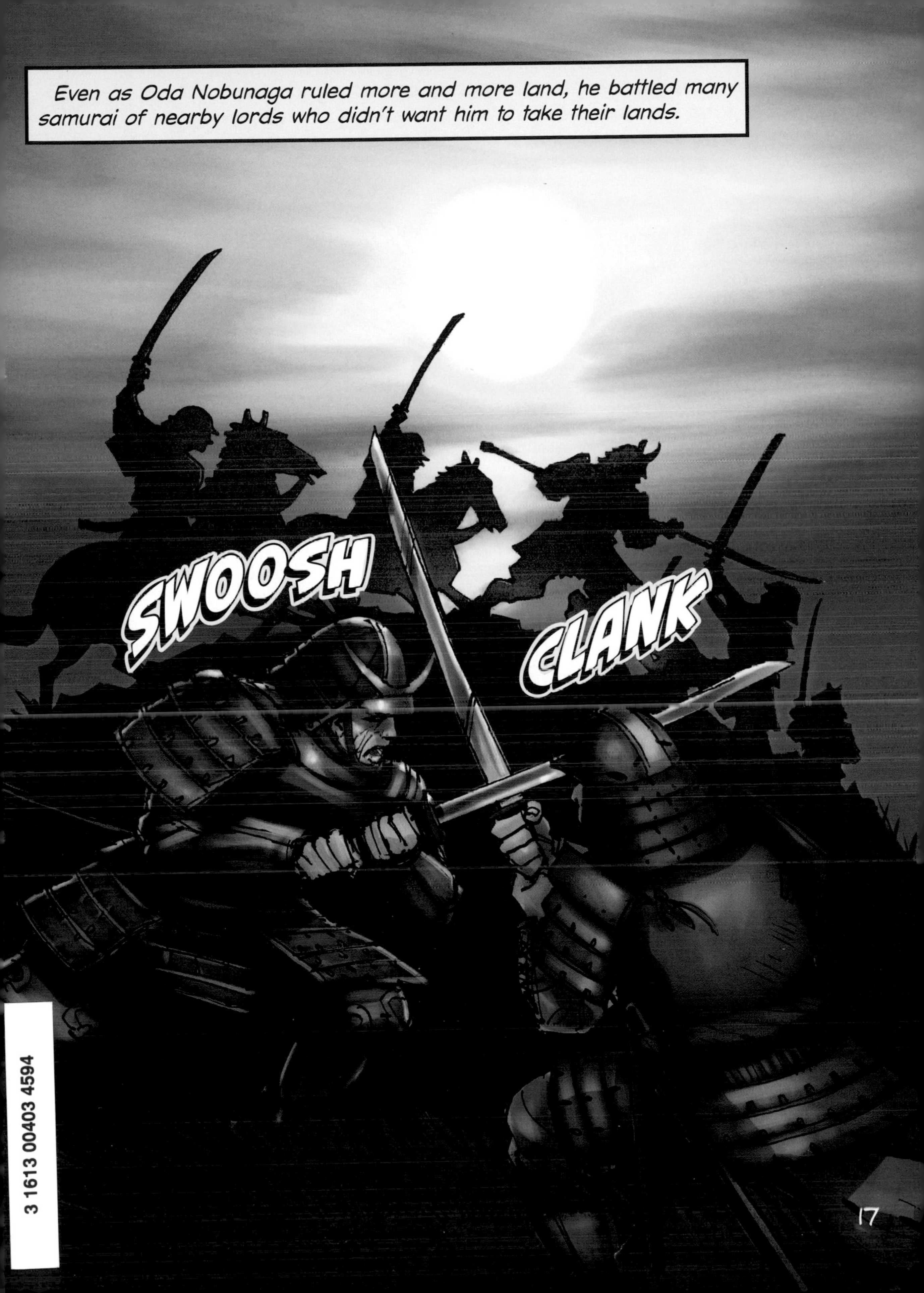
Even as Oda Nobunaga ruled more and more land, he battled many samurai of nearby lords who didn't want him to take their lands.
SWOOSH
CLANK

SAMURAI BATTLES

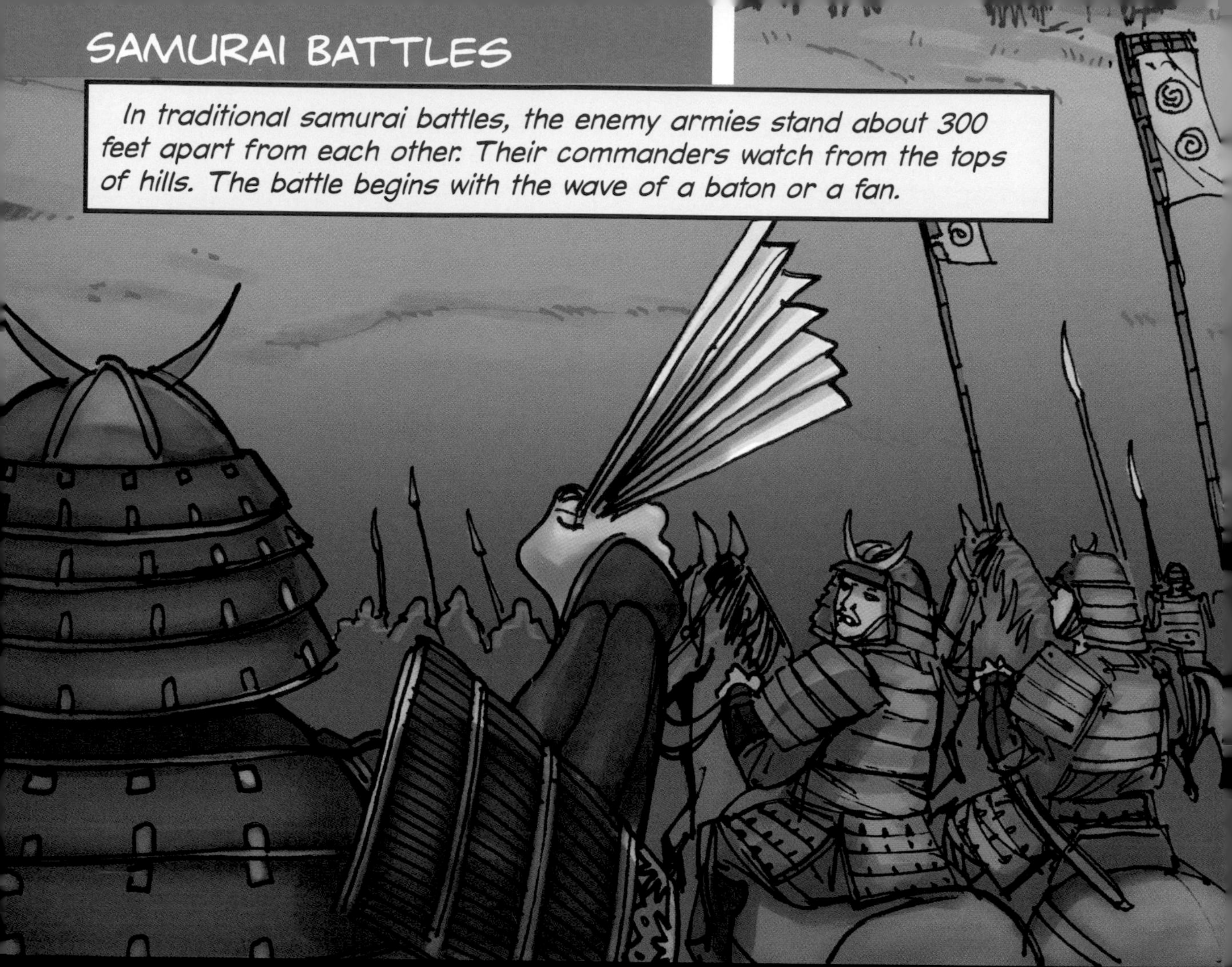
In traditional samurai battles, the enemy armies stand about 300 feet apart from each other. Their commanders watch from the tops of hills. The battle begins with the wave of a baton or a fan.

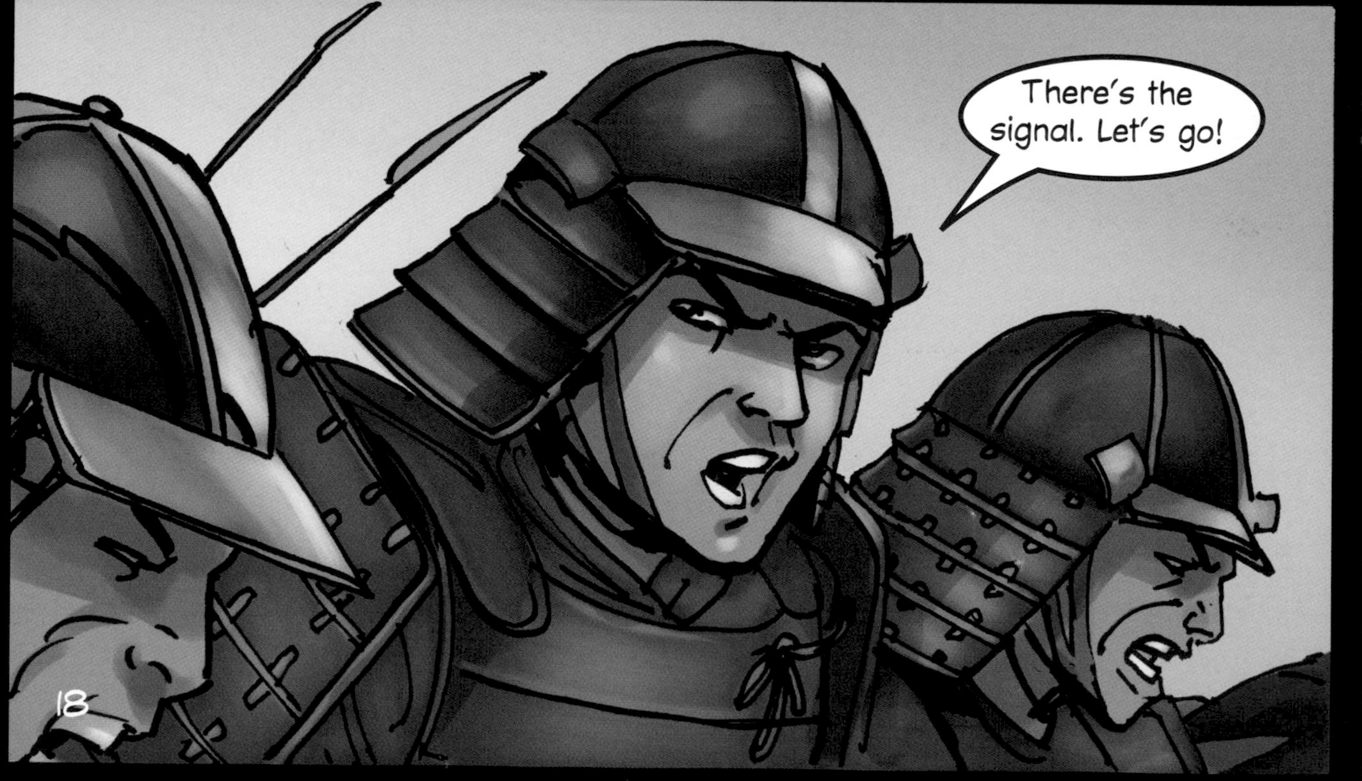
There's the signal. Let's go!

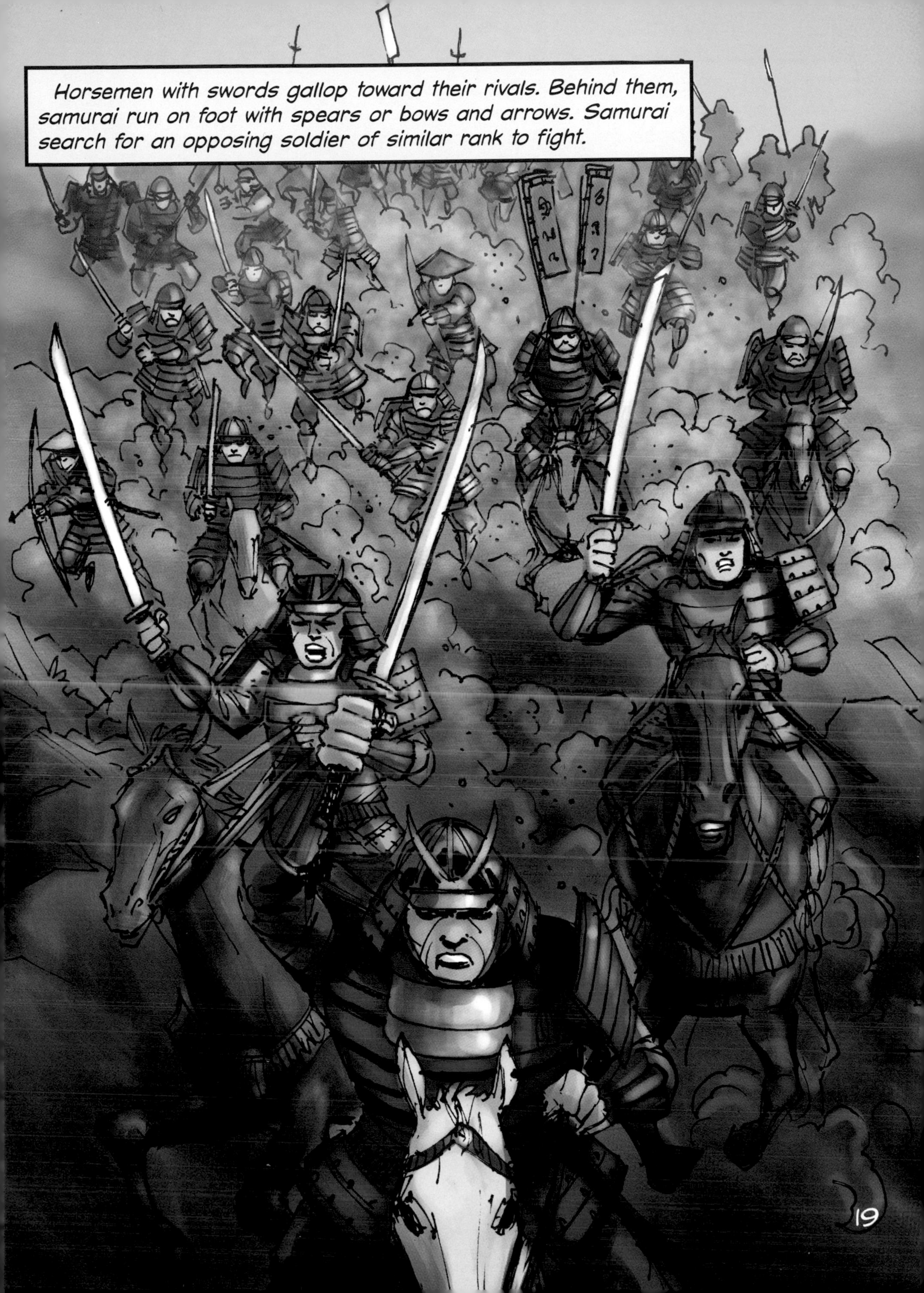
Horsemen with swords gallop toward their rivals. Behind them, samurai run on foot with spears or bows and arrows. Samurai search for an opposing soldier of similar rank to fight.

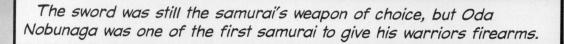

The sword was still the samurai's weapon of choice, but Oda Nobunaga was one of the first samurai to give his warriors firearms.

We can't get close enough to fight them with swords!

This changes everything! Those guns will kill us all if we don't run way.

20

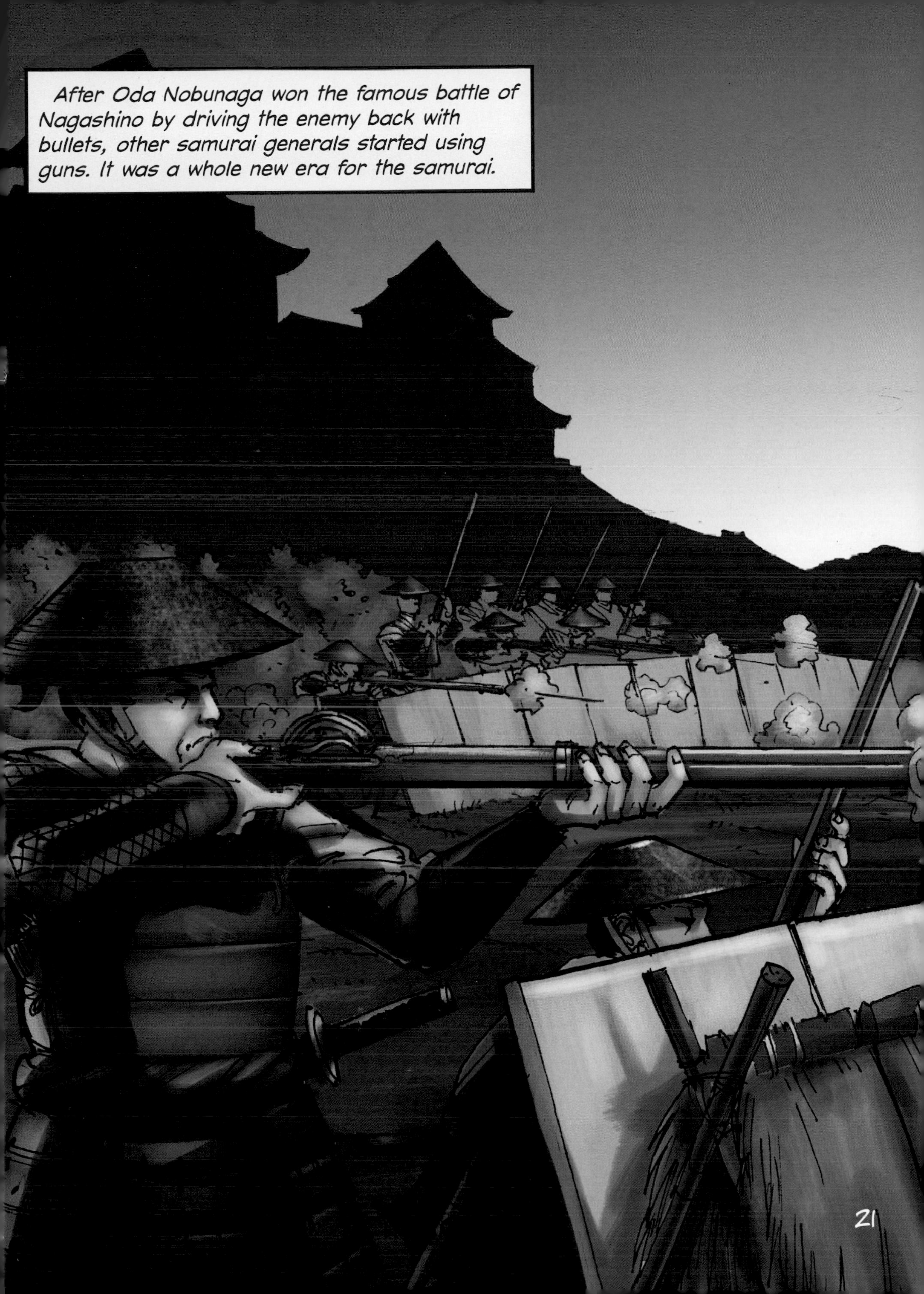
After Oda Nobunaga won the famous battle of Nagashino by driving the enemy back with bullets, other samurai generals started using guns. It was a whole new era for the samurai.

Along with Hideyoshi, Akechi Mitsuhide became one of Oda Nobunaga's most trusted samurai. He was both a general and a poet.
You two are my most trusted generals. I know you would never turn on me.

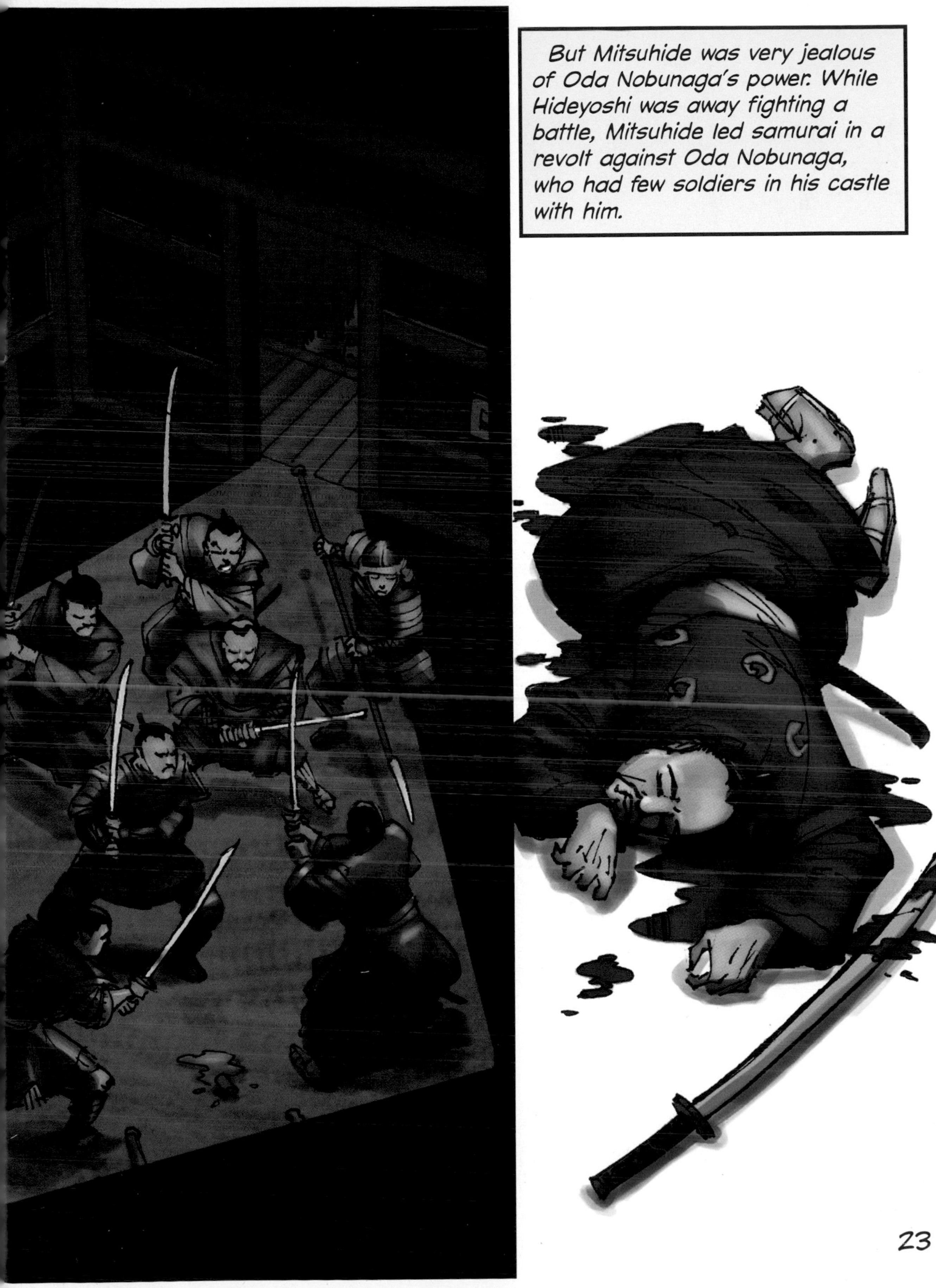
But Mitsuhide was very jealous of Oda Nobunaga's power. While Hideyoshi was away fighting a battle, Mitsuhide led samurai in a revolt against Oda Nobunaga, who had few soldiers in his castle with him.

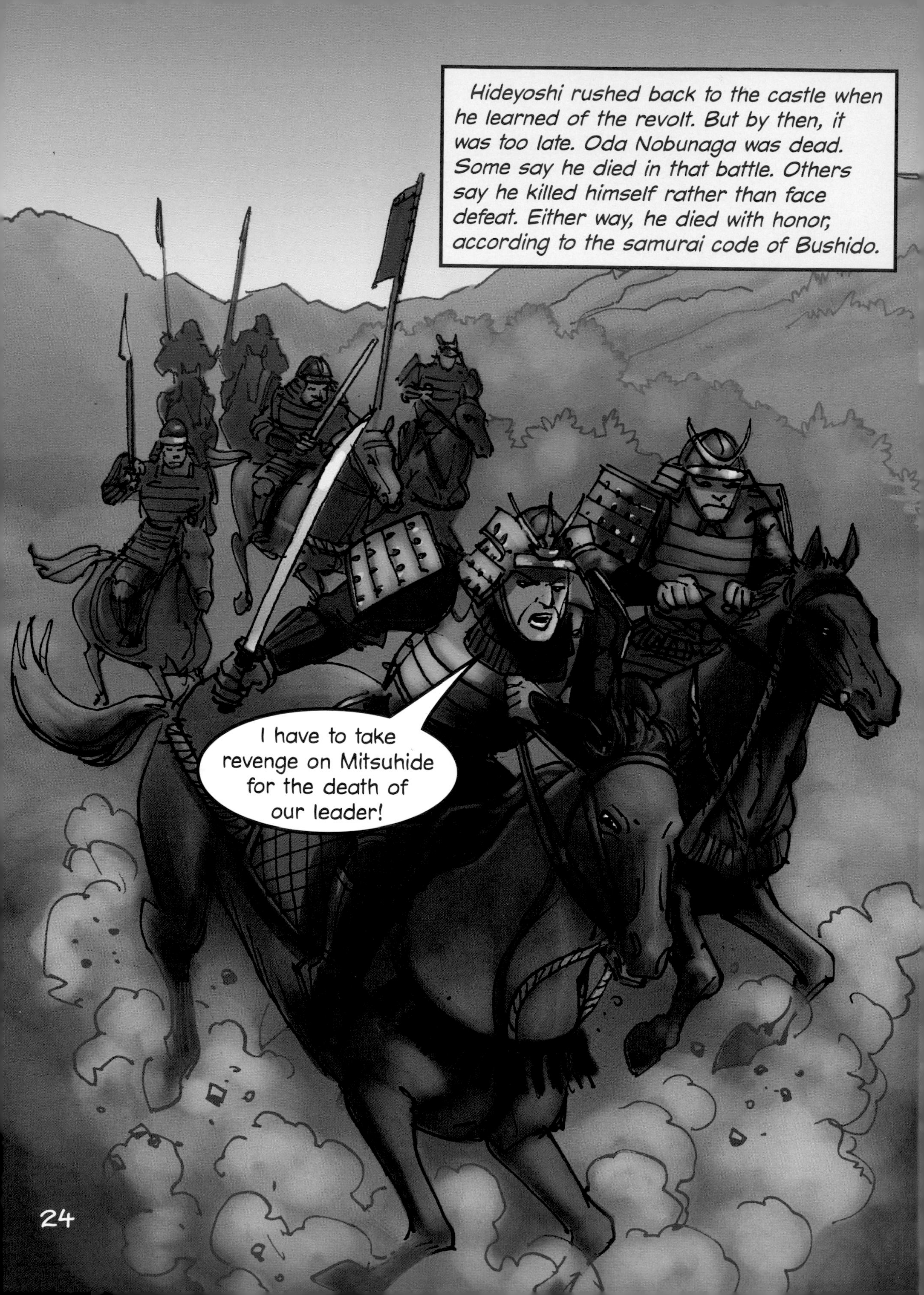
Hideyoshi rushed back to the castle when he learned of the revolt. But by then, it was too late. Oda Nobunaga was dead. Some say he died in that battle. Others say he killed himself rather than face defeat. Either way, he died with honor, according to the samurai code of Bushido.
I have to take revenge on Mitsuhide for the death of our leader!

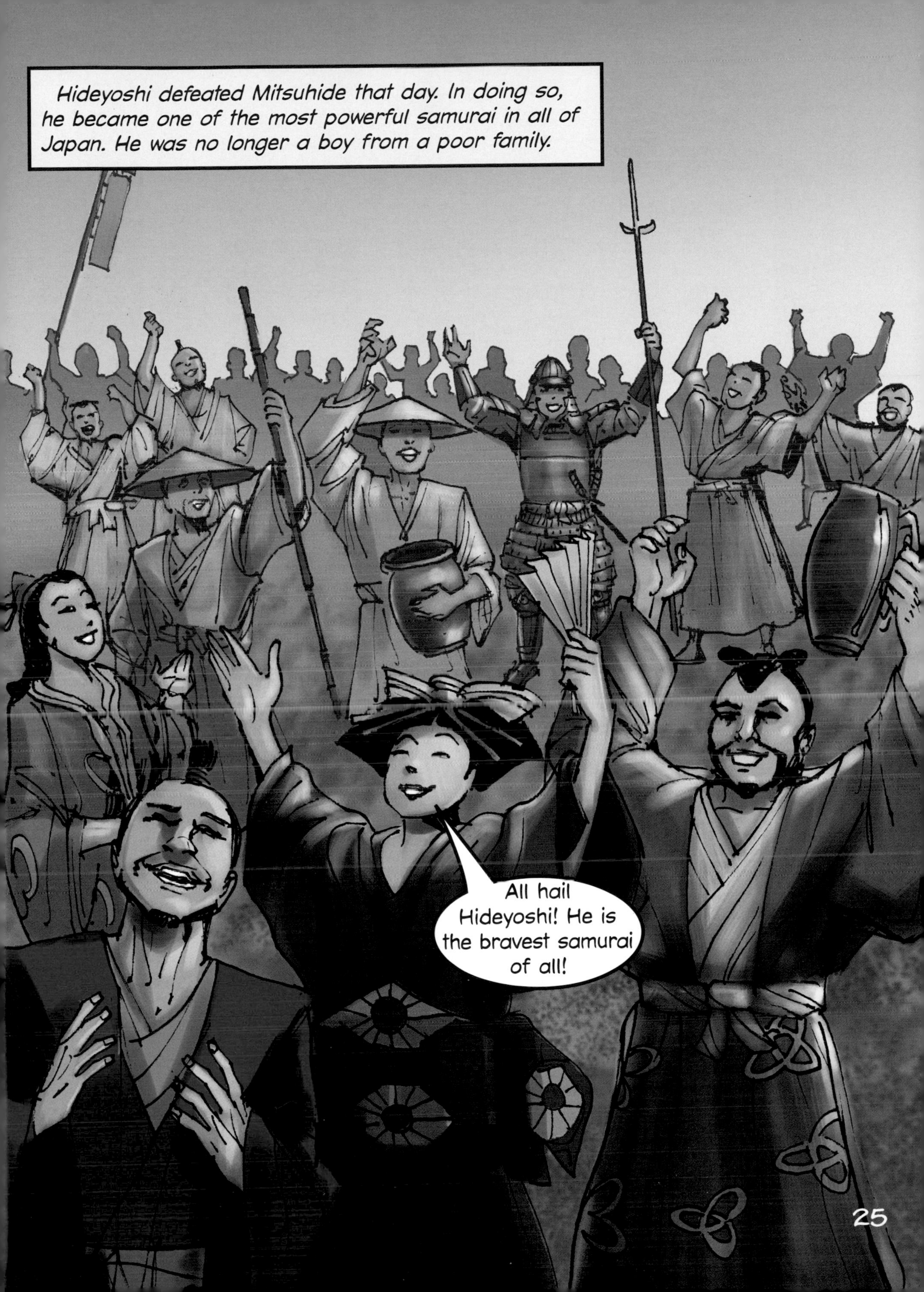
Hideyoshi defeated Mitsuhide that day. In doing so, he became one of the most powerful samurai in all of Japan. He was no longer a boy from a poor family.
All hail Hideyoshi! He is the bravest samurai of all!

Samurai History

Samurai were the noble warrior class of Japan, and they were also among the best educated of Japanese citizens. Some of them were poets and philosophers, while others studied art and history. Their most important role in society was to serve their master,

The son of a samurai, Matsuo Bahso (1644-1694) became a great **haiku** poet.

particularly in times of battle. When wars started, there was no time to study.

For as many as 1,500 years, the samurai played a major role in Japanese society. It is hard to tell how far back in history the samurai tradition began, but there is some evidence of this warrior class as early as the 5th century. The samurai gained in power and prestige as Japan developed into a society of masters who lived far from cities and whose land was protected by these warriors.

Samurai Armor and Weapons

To protect themselves when fighting, samurai wore heavy metal armor and iron helmets. They always carried two swords. One was long and curved. The other was shorter and broader. They also used bows and arrows, and blades attached to long poles. If they were beaten in battle, they might end their own lives, because death was more honorable than defeat.

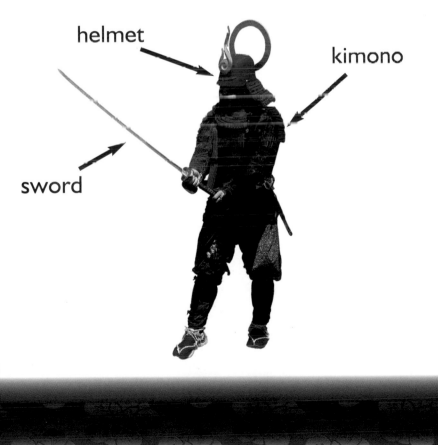

helmet

kimono

sword

The end of the samurai tradition came in 1876. More and more Japanese had been moving to the cities, and there weren't as

The Satsuma clan (from an 1860s photo) was one of the last of the great samurai families.

many powerful masters whose land needed protecting. The emperor put an end to the tradition by replacing the samurai with a national army. From then on, the samurai warrior culture was against the law.

Samurai History

Martial arts, such as **jujitsu** and **judo**, originated in Japan and are based on the practices of samurai warriors. Jujitsu emphasizes the combative practices of the samurai, in contrast to Judo, which focuses on meditation and very skillful techniques of self-defense.

WEBSITES

www.asianhistory.about.com/od/warsinasia/p/ SamuraiProfile.htm

www.samurai-archives.com/index.html

www.people.howstuffworks.com/samurai

www.enchantedlearning.com/crafts/origami

GLOSSARY

Bushido (BUSH-ih-doh): This is the way of the warrior. It is better to die than to disgrace yourself in defeat. Bushi means warrior, and do means way.

clan (klan): This is an extended family or large group of families.

firearm (FIRE-arm): This is any weapon that shoots bullets, such as a gun or a rifle.

haiku (hy-KOO): This is a short, three-line Japanese poem that doesn't rhyme. It has 17 syllables. There are five syllables in the first line, seven syllables in the second line, and five syllables in the third line.

helmet (HEL-mit): This is a hard covering for the head that protects it during battle or sports.

jujitsu (joo-JIT-soo): This is a form of fighting that came before judo and has many of the same techniques. It means the art of softness in Japanese.

judo (JOO-doh): This is a sport and fighting technique that originated in the samurai era. It means the easy way in Japanese and uses the other fighter's strength against him.

kimono (kuh-MOH-nuh): This is a colorful robe with wide sleeves and a sash for a belt. The kimono is mainly worn by women in modern Japan, but it is also worn by samurai.

samurai (SAM-oo-rye): This is a Japanese warrior. The word means those who serve in Japanese.

sword (sord): This is a weapon with a handle and a blade that is longer than a knife's blade.

INDEX

ABOUT THE AUTHOR

Don McLeese is a journalism professor at the University of Iowa. He has written many articles for newspapers and magazines and many books for young students as well.

ABOUT THE ARTIST

Chris Marrinan is an artist who has created images for many things, including everything from billboards to video game covers! He got his start in the comic book business drawing for comic book publishers DC Comics, Marvel, Dark Horse, and Image. Chris has drawn many comic icons, such as Wonder Woman, Spider-Man, and Wolverine. He lives in Northern California with his two children.